JUST BEING HAPPY

JUST BEING HAPPY

EDITED BY EDWIN GROVER

LAUGHING ELEPHANT BOOKS SEATTLE 2000

JUST BEING HAPPY

A reprint of a book originally published
by P.F. Volland and Company in 1912.

ISBN 1-883211-28-x

Laughing Elephant Books
Post Office Box 4399   Seattle Washington   98104

WHEN the makers of the constitution of the United States declared that "Life, Liberty and the pursuit of Happiness, were inalienable rights, they were voicing sentiments as old as humanity itself. Last but not least of these is "the pursuit of Happiness." To have life and liberty without happiness is to live an incomplete and unsatisfied life. Not that we ever attain complete happiness in this world—the pleasure comes in the pursuit, not in the attainment! Robert Louis Stevenson has truthfully said that "To travel hopefully is a better thing than to arrive."

One reason why we never overtake Happiness is because it is always fleeing from us. Only when we attain our ideal do we attain complete happiness, and as our ideals constantly recede, so Happiness in its complete fulfillment forever escapes us. But the pursuit of Happiness is the supreme joy in life and the sign that our faith is still strong and our hearts still young. Not dissatisfied but forever unsatisfied is the deathless cry of all human hearts.

One great inspiration to happy living is happy thinking, and this "Little Bundle of Happy Thoughts" is bound up in the hope that it may serve as a companion to those who love life and still pursue the blue bird of Happiness.

JUST being happy is a fine thing to do;
Looking on the bright side rather than the blue;
   Sad or sunny musing
   Is largely in the choosing,
And just being happy is brave work and true.

Just being happy helps other souls along;
Their burdens may be heavy and they not strong;
   And your own sky will lighten,
   If other skies you brighten
By just being happy with a heart full of song.

          —Ripley D. Saunders

WHAT does the lark in the meadow sing?
   "Be glad;"
What is the robin caroling?
   "Be glad;"
What are the words that the breezes bring
Over the hills, and what is the thing
That is sung by the rushes beside the spring?
Listen—the song of the breeze and birds
Is a song of joy that has two brave words:
   "Be glad."

          —S. E. Kiser

I'LL not confer with sorrow
  Till tomorrow;
  But Joy shall have her way
  This very day.

—T. B. Aldrich

TALK HAPPINESS

TALK happiness. The world is sad enough
Without your woe. No path is wholly rough.
Look for the places that are smooth and clear,
And speak of them to rest the weary ear
Of earth; so hurt by one continuous strain
Of mortal discontent and grief and pain.

Talk faith. The world is better off without
Your uttered ignorance and morbid doubt—
If you have faith in God, or man, or self,
Say so; if not, push back upon the shelf
Of silence all your thoughts till faith shall come;
No one will grieve because your lips are dumb.

Talk health. The dreary, never-ending tale
Of mortal maladies is worn and stale
You cannot charm, or interest, or please
By harping on that minor chord, disease.
Say you are well, or all is well with you,
And God shall hear your words, and make them true.

—Ella Wheeler Wilcox

BE happy; let who will be sad,
There are so many pleasant things,
So many things to make us glad,—
The flower that buds, the bird that sings;
And sweeter still than all of these
Are friendship and old memories.

—M. C. D

HAPPINESS grows at our own firesides, and is not to be picked in strangers' gardens.

—Douglas Jerrold

IF you want to be happy yourself, make others happy. If you want to make others happy, be first happy yourself. There you have the whole formula.

—Ossian Lang

ACQUIRE the habit of expecting success, or believing in happiness. Nothing succeeds like success; nothing makes happiness like happiness.

—Lilian Whiting

DON'T never pay t' go lookin' fer trouble—it's tew easy t' find. There ain't no sech thing's trouble 'n this world 'less ye look fer it. Happiness won't hev nuthin' t' dew with a man thet likes trouble. 'Minnit a man stops lookin' fer trouble happiness'll look fer him.

—Irving Bacheller

OBEY; be loyal; do your work and do it well. This is the message of nature, and the man cannot be long unhappy who imitates Nature's examples.

—Newell Dwight Hillis

FATE used me meanly and I looked at her and laughed,
That none might know how bitter was the cup I quaffed;
Along came Joy and paused beside me where I sat,
Saying, "I came to see what you were laughing at!"

—Ella Wheeler Wilcox

HAPPINESS comes not from the power of possession, but from the power of appreciation. Above most other things it is wise to cultivate the powers of appreciation. The greater the number of stops in an organ, the greater its possibilities as an instrument of music.

—H. W. Sylvester

THE art of being happy lies in the power of extracting happiness from common things.

—Henry Ward Beecher

TRUE happiness consists not in the multitude of friends, but in their worth and choice.

—Ben Jonson

WHAT ripeness is to the orange, what sweet song is to the lark, what culture and refinement are to the intellect, that happiness is to man.

—Newell Dwight Hillis

RULES FOR HAPPINESS

SOMETHING to do,
Some one to love,
Something to hope for.

—Kant

HAPPINESS is a condition attained through worthiness. To find your life you must lose it. It is the law and the prophets.

—Lilian Whiting

WE were made to radiate the perfume of good cheer and happiness as much as a rose was made to radiate its sweetness to every passerby.

THE happiness of your life depends upon the character of your thoughts.

—Marcus Aurelius

FOR every happy smile, the world
Whirls on its way with less of care.

IF you ever find happiness by hunting for it, you will find it as
the old woman did her lost spectacles, safe on her own nose all
the time.

—Josh Billings

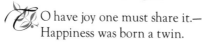

TO have joy one must share it.—
Happiness was born a twin.

—Byron

GENEROSITY is the investment from which we clip the
coupons of happiness.

—Four Track News

BLESSED are the happiness makers.

—Henry Ward Beecher

HALF the world is on the wrong scent in the pursuit of happiness. They think it consists in having and getting, and in being
served by others. It consists in giving and in serving others.

—Henry Drummond

WHAT do we live for if it is not to make life less difficult for others?

—George Eliot

BE cheerful. Give this lonesome world a smile.
We stay at longest but a little while.
Hasten we must, or we shall lose the chance
To give the gentle word, the kindly glance.
Be sweet and tender—that is doing good;
'Tis doing what no other kind deed could.

THE unpardonable sin in a mother is gloom. If you would influence your children for good, let your presence radiate smiles. Let your children hear you laugh often; but laugh with them, never at them.

—Gladys Harvey-Knight

WOULD'ST contentment thou keep within thy heart?
Then care not what thou hast, but what thou art.
And keep thee true to what is best in thee,
And true to her thou lovest; pray that she
May love thee, too. Then laugh at all the rest;
No other God need'st thou; thou hast the best.

—Cleveland Moffett

*H*APPINESS is the only good. The place to be happy is here. The time to be happy is now. The way to be happy is to make others so.

—Robert G. Ingersoll

*H*ARMONY at the center radiates happiness throughout the whole sphere of life.

*O*NE makes one's own happiness only by taking care of the happiness of others.

—Bernardin de Saint-Pierre

*M*AKE one person happy each day and in forty years you have made 14,600 human beings happy for a little time at least.

*I*S it not the first duty of those who are happy to tell of their gladness to others? All men can learn to be happy; and the teaching of it is easy.

—Maurice Maeterlinck

*T*HERE is no satisfaction comparable to that of making one's neighbor happy.

—Mme. d'Epinay

EACH day still better others' happiness,
Until the heavens, enjoying earth's good hap,
Add an immortal title to your crown!
—Shakespeare

THE discovery of a new dish makes more for the happiness of man than the discovery of a star.

NOT what we have, but what we use;
Not what we see, but what we choose—
These are the things that mar or bless
The sum of human happiness.

IF I am happy in spite of my deprivations, if my happiness is so deep that it is a faith, so thoughtful that it becomes a philosophy of life,—my testimony to the creed of optimism is worth hearing. My optimism rests on a glad belief in the preponderance of good and a willing effort always to co-operate with the good, that it may prevail. I try to increase the power God has given me to see the best in everything and every one, and make that best a part of my life.

WE communicate happiness to others not often by great acts of devotion and self-sacrifice, but by the absence of fault-finding and censure, by being ready to sympathize with their notions and feelings, instead of forcing them to sympathize with ours.

—James Freeman Clarke

STRENGTH is success. Strength to be, strength to do, strength to love, strength to live. It is not happiness, it is not amusement, it is not content. These will come but they are not the object.

—Edward Everett Hale

TO be truly happy is a question of how we begin and not of how we end, of what we want and not of what we have.

—Robert Louis Stevenson

LIFE is for character, it is to be lived and lived happily, and everything should be put aside that is not essential to the one thing, namely, more life, more thoughts and higher, more hours of noble emotion and deeper ones, more friendships and purer.

—Newell Dwight Hillis

A LAUGH is worth one hundred groans in any market.

—Charles Lamb

HAPPINESS does not come in boulders generally, but in pebbles, so I think we all ought to be thankful when we receive such a pebble; and how much more delightful to give one!

—Gail Hamilton

DON'T fail to make your smile your children's last memory as they depart for school. A ruffled spirit as a send-off puts the tune out of joint for the entire day. Don't forget that you are, or ought to be, your children's ideal of all that is perfection, and that it is your duty to live up to those ideals in every possible way. Not an easy task, but wonderfully inspiring.

—Mrs. G. E. Jackson

A PLACID face and a gentle tone will make my family more happy than anything else I can do for them.

—E. T. King

THERE is no abiding happiness away from effort.

—J. Brierley

CHARACTER is the basis of happiness, and happiness is the sanction of character.

HAPPINESS is purely a matter of reciprocity. He who is happiest is he who gives the most happiness.

IT is a matter of economy to be happy, to view life and all its conditions from the brightest angle. It enables one to seize life at its best.

—Horatio W. Dresser

HAPPINESS is a perfume you cannot pour on others without getting a few drops yourself.

THE secret of happiness is not in doing what one likes, But in liking what one has to do.

—Barrie

THERE is no duty we so much underrate as the duty of being happy. By being happy we sow anonymous benefits upon the world, which remain unknown even to ourselves, or when they are disclosed, surprise nobody so much as the benefactor.

—Robert Louis Stevenson

CHEERFUL comrade is better than a waterproof coat and a foot-warmer.

—Henry van Dyke

HEERFULNESS and content are great beautifiers and are famous preservers of youthful looks.

—Charles Dickens

E are not simple enough to be happy and to render others so. We lack the singleness of heart and the self forgetfulness.

—Charles Wagner

RUE happiness is to no place confined,
But yet is found in a contented mind.

HE foundation of abiding happiness is one's chosen life work.

—Newell Dwight Hillis

T is the German thinker, Carl Hilty, who has so aptly written that in our frenzied search after happiness in this twentieth century, "the art of life is lost in the pace of living."

—G. H. K.

HAPPY, happier far than thou
With the laurel on thy brow,
She that makes the humblest hearth
Lovely to but one on earth.

—Felicia Dorothea Hemans

IF one would be happy, let him forget himself and go about making some one else happy.

—Lilian Whiting

BEFORE we can bring happiness to others, we must first be happy ourselves; nor will happiness abide with us unless we confer it on others.

—Maurice Maeterlinck

MAY each year be happier than the last, and not the meanest of our brethren or sisterhood debarred their rightful share in what the Great Creator formed them to enjoy.

—Charles Dickens

TO be happy is only to have freed one's soul from the unrest of unhappiness.

—Maurice Maeterlinck

THE human heart is large enough to contain any amount of happiness.

—T. W. Robertson

HAPPINESS depends on helpfulness as health depends on air and food. They who are intent on ministration, looking for opportunities to be of service to their neighbors, find the dullest places interesting. The unselfish person lives in an environment of happiness, surrounded by those whom he has helped to be happy, and who in return are endeavoring to bring happiness to him.

—George Hodges

THE HAPPINESS OF HELPFULNESS

STEVENSON speaks of "the great task of happiness." But happiness is not a task. It is not even an occupation. It is a quality of life. Happiness depends on helpfulness. That's the reason joy is social. Helpfulness keeps happiness because it adds to the area of affection. People are not happy when they seek after happiness. They become steeped in happiness when they undertake to promote the joy of others.

—Walter Williams

LET any clever woman simply take it to heart to make everybody about her as happy as she can, and the result will always be wonderful.

HAVE you not sometimes seen happiness? Yes, the happiness of others.

—Arsene Houssaye

*I*F you can help anybody even a little, be glad; up the steps of usefulness and kindness, God will lead you on to happiness and friendship.

—Maltbie Babcock

OBEYING THE HEAVENLY VISION

*W*E can't choose happiness. We can only choose whether we will indulge ourselves in the present moment or whether we will renounce that for the sake of obeying the divine voice within us—for the sake of being true to all the motives that sanctify our lives. I know this belief is hard but I have felt that if I let it go forever, I should have no light through the darkness of this life.

—George Eliot

INDITE THE BEST THOUGHTS

*T*HE secret of happiness is to want the best things and to want them very much.

—F. G. Peabody

IDEALS FOR THOUGHTS

*T*HAT man is the happiest who has the most interesting things to think about.

—Timothy Dwight

OUR happiness today is to so enormous an extent in our own hands. A man is happy when he thinks he is. And why should I not this morning think so? Why should I be gloomy when I can be glad? Here inside me is a force that can drive away the clouds. Our will power, which can call up good thoughts and disperse bad ones; which can fall back on gracious memories as a refuge from present evils; which, in a word, can make its own weather—our will power, if we will only use it, is our philosopher's stone, that turns all things into gold. The more we give it to do, the better it works.

—J. Brierley

THERE is a beautiful and an ugly way in which to say almost everything, and happiness depends upon which way we take. You can upset a person for the whole day by the harsh way in which you may call him in the morning, or you may give him a beautiful start by the cheeriness of your greeting. So not only in words but in all the little, common courtesies and duties of life, think of the beautiful way of doing each.

—Delia L. Porter

JUST to fill the hour—that is happiness. Fill my hour, ye gods, so that I shall not say, whilst I have done this, "Behold, also, an hour of my life is gone"—but rather, "I have lived an hour."

—Emerson

THERE is no difference between one person and another more characteristic and noticeable than the facility of being happy. Some seem pierced with half a hundred windows, through which stream warmth, light and sounds of delight. It comes in at the eye and at the ear, at the portals of smell, taste, and touch, in things little and great.

—Henry Ward Beecher

IF all could realize the power of even a small pleasure, how much happier the world would be! And how much longer bodies and souls both would bear up under living! Sensitive people realize that often it happens to them to be revived, kindled, strengthened to a degree which they could not describe, by some little thing—some word of praise, some token of remembrance, some proof of affection or recognition.

—Helen Hunt Jackson

A LITTLE thought will show you how vastly your own happiness depends on the way other people bear themselves toward you. Turn the idea around, and remember that just so much are you adding to the pleasure or the misery of other people's days.

—George S. Merriam

BLESSED are they who are pleasant to live with.

TO dwell happily together, they should be versed in the niceties of the heart, and born with a faculty for willing compromise.

—Robert Louis Stevenson

THERE is nothing like putting the shine on another's face to put the shine on our own. Nine-tenths of all loneliness, sensitiveness, despondency, moroseness, are connected with personal interests. Turn more of these selfish interests into unselfish ones, and by so much we change opportunities for disheartenment into their opposite.

—W. C. Gannett

MENTAL sunshine makes the mind grow, and perpetual happiness makes human nature a flower garden in bloom.

—Christian D. Larson

HAPPY WAYS OF DOING THINGS

THERE is always a best way of doing everything, if it be but to boil an egg. Manners are the happy ways of doing things, each one a stroke of genius or of love, now repeated and hardened with usage. . . . You cannot rightly train one to an air and manner, except by making him the kind of man of whom that manner is the natural expression. Nature forever puts a premium on reality. What is done for effect is seen to be done for effect.

—Emerson

DO not keep the alabaster box of your love and friendship sealed up until your friends are dead. Fill their lives with sweetness. Speak approving, cheering words while their ears can hear them, and while their hearts can be thrilled and made happier. The kind things you mean to say when they are gone, say before they go.

—George W. Childs

THE happy person is the one who finds occasions for joy at every step. He does not have to look for them, he just finds them.

—Ossian

WHO that define it, say they more or less
Than this—that happiness is happiness?

—Pope

THE great secret of happiness is to study to accommodate our own minds to things external rather than to accommodate things external to ourselves.

—Dugald Stewart

BE sure to live on the sunny side, and even then do not expect the world to look bright, if you habitually wear gray-brown glasses.

—Charles W. Eliot

SOW thou sorrow and thou shalt reap it, Sow thou joy and thou shalt keep it.

—Richard Watson Gilder

ALL these are elements of happiness—love of nature, acquaintance with the wide earth, congenial intercourse with superior minds, and abiding friendships.

—Charles W. Eliot

IF thou workest at that which is before thee, following right reason seriously, vigorously, calmly, without allowing anything else to distract thee, but keeping thy divine part pure, if thou shouldst be bound to give it back immediately; if thou holdest to this, expecting nothing, fearing nothing, but satisfied with thy present activity according to nature, and with heroic truth in every word and sound which thou utterest, thou wilt live happy. And there is no man who is able to prevent this.

—Marcus Aurelius

IF your whole world is upside down and joy and cheer are far from you, romp for an hour with a six-year old child and see if its laughter and faith are not veritable sign posts on The Road to Happiness.

—Gladys Harvey-Knight

WOULD ye learn the road to Laughtertown,
O ye who have lost the way?
Would ye have young heart though your hair be gray?
Go learn from a little child each day,
Go serve his wants and play his play,
And catch the lilt of his laughter gay,
And follow his dancing feet as they stray;
For he knows the road to Laughtertown,
O ye who have lost the way.

—Katherine D. Blake

IT pays to be happy. Happiness is not a luxury, but a necessity. The beneficial effect of mental sunshine on life, ability, strength, vitality, endurance, is most pronounced.

—Christian D. Larson

IN the long run, people are generally apt to get what they look for; those who are seeking trouble usually find it. A happy disposition is therefore to be cultivated.

—Henry D. Chapin

THERE are two things which will make us happy in this life, if we attend to them. The first is, never to vex ourselves about what we cannot help; and the second, never to vex ourselves about what we can help.

—Chatfield

THE happy have whole days, and those they use;
Th' unhappy have but hours, and those they lose.

—Dryden

I FIND the gayest castles in the air that were ever piled far better for comfort and for use than the dungeons in the air that are daily dug and caverned out by grumbling, discontented people. A man should make life and nature happier to us, or he had better never been born.

—Emerson

THE measure of a man's happiness will be the number and strength of his friendships among people young and people old, people rich and people poor, people representing professions and those representing the occupations.

—Newell Dwight Hillis

HAPPINESS appears to be a state that comes easiest when unsought.

—Henry D. Chapin

BECAUSE God is doing the best He can for all, in the very darkest hour of life, happiness and tranquillity are possible for all alike.

—Newell Dwight Hillis

THE best way to secure future happiness is to be as happy as is rightfully possible today.

—Charles W. Eliot

THE domestic affections are the principal sources of human happiness and well-being.

—Charles W. Eliot

FOR to what can happiness be wisely sacrificed but to greater happiness?

—John Hawkesworth

IT is better than a sermon to hear my wife Prue talk to the children; and when she speaks to me it seems sweeter than psalm singing; at least, such as we have in our church. I am very happy.

—George William Curtis

BE glad of life, because it gives you the chance to love and to work and to play and to look up at the stars.

—Henry van Dyke

WHAT we need is, not more cultivation, but a recognized habit of enjoyment.

—Agnes Repplier

HAPPINESS is the most accommodating of all things. It will come to a cottage as soon as to a palace. You need never wait for any outward pomp to come. As the sunshine of the Almighty will shine through a simple vine as richly as upon the velvet of a king or upon the gilded dome of a temple, so happiness falls with equal sweetness upon all whose minds are at peace and in whose hearts flow the good thoughts and good sentiments of life.

—David Swing

YOU are very sensible how much you have rambled after happiness and failed. Neither learning, nor wealth, nor fame, nor pleasure could ever help you to it. Which way is it to be had, then? By acting up to the height of human nature. And how shall a man do this? Why, by getting a right set of principles for impulses and action.

—Marcus Aurelius

JOY is the very distilled elixir of energy and inspiration. It is the most invincible force. It is the power which is able to conquer and prevail.

—Lilian Whiting

IF a man is unhappy, this must be his own fault; for God made all men to be happy.

—Epictetus

MISERY is the exception, happiness is the rule. No rational man ever heard a bird sing without feeling that the bird was happy, and that if God made that bird He made it to be happy, and He takes pleasure in its happiness, though no human heart should ever share in its joy.

—Charles Kingsley

IF you want knowledge, you must toil for it; and if pleasure, you must toil for it. Toil is the law. Pleasure comes through toil, and not by self-indulgence and indolence. When one gets to love work, his life is a happy one.

—John Ruskin

THE only happiness a brave man ever troubled himself with asking much about was happiness enough to get his work done. Not "I can't eat!" but "I can't work!"—that was the burden of all wise complaining among men. It is, after all, the one unhappiness of a man—that he cannot work.

—Thomas Carlyle

HAPPINESS is not like a large and beautiful gem, so uncommon and rare that all search for it is in vain, all efforts to obtain it hopeless; but it consists of a series of smaller and commoner gems, grouped and set together, forming a pleasing and graceful whole.

—Samuel Smiles

ND now you are to ask yourself if, when all is done, it would not have been better to sit by the fire at home, and be happy thinking. To sit still and contemplate—to remember the faces of women without desire, to be pleased by the great deeds of men without envy, to be everything and everywhere in sympathy, and yet content to remain where and what you are—is not this to know both wisdom and virtue, and to dwell with happiness?

—Walking Tours

OW it blesses the street, a face laughing all to itself! As soon as one sees it, the corners of his mouth begin to twitch, too, with the God's gift. Eyes light, strangers greet knowingly, hearts soften, spirits rise, lives brighten, and the world grows friendly, within the circle of the merry echo. Educate your laugh, if you can, to ring often and sweet, that you may be able to radiate widely your pleasure and health. If we may judge by the abundance of the glad sound, and its rapid radiation around every source of it, a good time must be part of the established success of Providence.

—William C. Gannet

HE happiest man is he who best understands his happiness, and he who understands it best is he who knows profoundly that his happiness is only divided from sorrow by a lofty, unwearying, humane and courageous view of life.

—Maurice Maeterlinck

T is only a poor sort of happiness that could ever come by caring very much about our own narrow pleasures. We can only have the highest happiness by having wide thoughts, and much feeling for the rest of the world as well as ourselves; and this sort of happiness often brings so much pain with it that we can only tell it from pain by its being what we would choose before everything else, because our souls see it is good.

—George Eliot

O give happiness and to do good, there is our only law, our anchor of salvation, our beacon light, our reason for existing. All religions may crumble away; so long as these survive we have still an ideal, and life is worth living.

—Amiel

HERE'S lots of fun in the world if a fellow only knows how to find it.

—Elliot Flower

O make any one happy is strictly to augment his store of being, to double the intensity of his life, to reveal him to himself, to ennoble him and transfigure him. Happiness does away with ugliness, and even makes the beauty of beauty. The man who doubts it can never have watched the first gleams of tenderness dawning in the clear eyes of one who loves—sunrise itself is a lesser marvel.

—Amiel

IS not making others happy the best happiness? To illuminate for an instant the depths of a deep soul, to cheer those who bear by sympathy the burden of so many sorrow laden hearts and suffering lives, is to me a blessing and a precious privilege. There is a sort of religious joy in helping to renew the strength and courage of noble minds. We are surprised to find ourselves the possessors of a power of which we are not worthy, and we long to exercise it purely and seriously.

—Amiel

LIFE is short, and we never have too much time for gladening the hearts of those who are traveling the dark journey with us. O be swift to love, make haste to be kind!

—Amiel

THERE can be no real and abiding happiness without sacrifice. Our greatest joys do not result from our efforts toward self-gratification, but from a loving and spontaneous service to other lives. Joy comes not to him who seeks it for himself, but to him who seeks it for other people.

—H. W. Sylvester

N such a world, so thorny, and where none
Finds happiness unblighted, or, if found,
Without some thistly sorrow at his side,
It seems the law of wisdom, and no sin
Against the law of love, to measure lots
With less distinguish'd than ourselves; that thus
We may with patience bear our moderate ills,
And sympathize with others suffering more.

—W. Cowper

E cannot have happiness until we forget to seek for it. We cannot find peace until we enter the path of self-sacrificing usefulness.

—Henry van Dyke

NE of Dr. Johnson's ingredients of happiness was, "A little less time than you want." That means always to have so many things you want to see, to have, and to do, that no day is quite long enough for all you think you would like to get done before you go to bed.

—Helen Hunt Jackson

ILIAN WHITING says that no one can be unhappy who is filled with interest in the happiness of others.

O be happy and make others happy is the highest duty and privilege in life. Ill temper is the chief of crimes and misdemeanors. Ill temper is contagious, and a person has no more right to go about scattering germs of bad temper than he has to propagate smallpox or the measles. "Sunshine from all and for all" is our home motto, and instant quarantine is the penalty for a failure to live up to it. I believe a happy disposition contributes more to success in a life career than any other single element.

—Dorothy Storrs

O one has any more right to go about unhappy than he has to go about ill-bred. He owes it to himself, to his friends, to society, and to the community in general, to live up to his best spiritual possibilities, not only now and then, once or twice a year, or once in a season, but every day and every hour.

—Lilian Whiting

APPINESS, at least, is not solitary; it joys to communicate; it loves others, for it depends on them for its existence; it sanctions and encourages to all delights that are not unkind in themselves. The very name and appearance of a happy man breathe of good-nature, and help the rest of us to live.

—Robert Louis Stevenson

CERTAIN simplicity of living is usually necessary to happiness.

—Henry D. Chapin

APPINESS is not in the possession of a fortune; happiness is in the self-reliance and industry that makes a fortune.

—Newell Dwight Hillis

NE'S birthright is happiness. It is as freely offered as the sunshine and the air. It is a spiritual state, and not conditioned by material limits.

—Lilian Whiting

APPINESS is inward, and not outward; and so it does not depend on what we have, but on what we are.

—Henry van Dyke

O believe and go forward is the key to success and to happiness.

—Lilian Whiting

HE world is so full of a number of things,
I'm sure we should all be as happy as kings.

—Robert Louis Stevenson

O be strong
Is to be happy!

—Henry W. Longfellow

THE first requisite for enduring happiness is in having work to do in which one believes.

—Henry D. Chapin

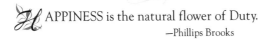

HAPPINESS is the natural flower of Duty.

—Phillips Brooks

THE unhappy are always wrong; wrong in being so, wrong in saying so, wrong in needing help of others.

BE pleasant until ten o'clock in the morning, and the rest of the day will take care of itself.

THERE is no happiness, then, but in a virtuous and self-approving conduct. Unless our actions will bear the test of our sober judgments and reflections upon them, they are not the actions, and, consequently, not the happiness of a rational being.

—Franklin

YOU have not fulfilled *every* duty unless you have fulfilled that of being pleasant.

—Charles Buxton

HAT happy state of mind, so rarely possessed, in which we can say, "I have enough," is the highest attainment of philosophy. Happiness consists, not in possessing much, but in being content with what we possess. He who wants little always has enough.

—Zimmerman

RESOLVE

O create happiness in myself and others. I will keep a strong body for the work I have to do; a loving heart for those about me; a clear mind for all truth, whose recognition brings freedom; a poised, unconquerable soul for the ideal whose champion I declare myself, and I will possess a faith mighty enough to rout anxiety, ride over difficulty, challenge hardship, smile through grief, deny failure, see only victory, looking to the end; by which hopeful assurance now attuned, I am at peace with myself, the world, and the Infinite.

O not forget that even as "to work is to worship," so to be cheery is to worship also; and to be happy is the first step to being pious.

—Robert Louis Stevenson

APPINESS is a very beautiful thing—the most beautiful and heavenly thing in the world.

—Lilian Whiting

PLEASURE, like all other truly precious things in this world, cannot be bought or sold. If you wish to be amused, you must do your part toward it; that is the essential.

—Charles Wagner

RECIPE FOR A HAPPY LIFE

THREE ounces are necessary, first of patience,
Then of repose and peace; of conscience
A pound entire is needful:
Of pastimes of all sorts, too,
Should be gathered as much as the hand can hold;
Of pleasant memory and of hope three good drachms
There must be at least. But they should moistened be
With a liquor made from true pleasures which rejoice the heart.
Then of love's magic drops a few—
But use them sparingly, for they may bring a flame
Which naught but tears can drown.
Grind the whole and mix therewith of merriment an ounce
To even. Yet all this may not bring happiness
Except in your orisons you lift your voice
To Him who holds the gift of health.

—Margaret of Navarre (1500)

TO live, we must conquer incessantly, we must have the courage to be happy.

—Amiel

TRUE happiness (if understood)
Consists alone in doing good.

—Somerville

SPEAKING of happiness, Joseph Jefferson once said: "My boys sometimes get discouraged and I say to them: 'Go out and do something for somebody. Go out and give something to anybody, if it's only a pair of woolen stockings to a poor old woman; it will take you away from yourself and make you happy!'"

 AM happy in having learned to distinguish between ownership and possession. Books, pictures, and all the beauty of the world belong to those who love and understand them—not usually to those who possess them. All of these things that I am entitled to I have—I own them by divine right. So I care not a bit who possesses them. I used to care very much and consequently was very unhappy.

—James Howard Kehler

THERE is an idea abroad among moral people that they should make their neighbors good. One person I have to make good: myself. But my duty to my neighbor is much more nearly expressed by saying that I have to make him happy—if I may.

—Robert Louis Stevenson

AKE Joy home,
And make a place in thy great heart for her;
Then will she come, and oft will sing to thee,
When thou art working in the furrows; aye,
Or weeding in the sacred hour of dawn.
It is a comely fashion to be glad—
Joy is the grace we say to God.

—Jean Ingelow

HE great lesson to be learned is that happiness is within us. No passing amusement, no companionship, no material possession can permanently satisfy. We must hoard up our own strength. We must depend upon our own resources for amusement and pleasure. We must make or mar our own tranquillity. To teach them this is the preparation for life which we can give our children.

HE real test of character is joy. For what you rejoice in, that you love and what you love, that you are like.

—Henry van Dyke

OMEWHERE on the great world the sun is always shining, and just so sure as you live, it will some time shine on you. The dear God has made it so. There is so much sunshine we must all have our share.

—Myrtle Reed

LESSED are the happiness makers! Blessed are they that take away attritions, that remove friction, that make the courses of life smooth, and the intercourse of men gentle!

—Henry Ward Beecher

HE first step toward happiness is to determine to be happy.

—George Hodges

S not making others happy the best happiness?

—Amiel

THE SECRET OF A HAPPY DAY

 TAKE it that in a happy day—and all life should be of one piece—there must be such a proportion between labor and rest or pleasure as shall leave a balance in favor of labor, so that one may have a permanent sense of achievement, without which there can be no solid sense of happiness, because it justifies human life.

—T. T. Munger

F I have faltered more or less
In my great task of happiness;
If I have moved among my race
And shown no glorious morning face;
If beams from happy human eyes
Have moved me not; if morning skies,
Books, and my food, and summer rain,
Knocked on my sullen heart in vain:—
Lord, Thy most pointed pleasure take
And stab my spirit broad awake;
Or, Lord, if too obdurate I,
Choose Thou, before that spirit die,
A piercing pain, a killing sin,
And to my dead heart run them in!

—Robert Louis Stevenson

HE best way to secure a happy home is to be happy yourself. One really happy person is enough to create a delightful, pervasive atmosphere of happiness. To have a happy home, set the example of self-sacrifice, love, service, of ministering rather than expecting to be ministered unto—and see what comes of it!

HOME in which no laughter is heard is only a house, after all; nay, worse, it is a tomb.

—G. H. Knight

WE may be sure that cheerful beliefs about the unseen world framed in full harmony with the beauty of the visible universe, and with the sweetness of domestic affections and joys, and held in company with kindred and friends, will illuminate the dark places on the pathway of earthly life and brighten all the road.

—Charles W. Eliot

OF all good gifts which ever came out of the wallet of the Fairy Godmother, the gift of natural gladness is the greatest and best. It is to the soul what health is to the body, what sanity is to the mind, the test of normality.

—Bliss Carman

HAPPINESS must not be left too much to outside conditions. The ultimate result of life will be ourselves—nothing more nor less. It is, after all, what we *are* that largely makes for contentment.

—Henry D. Chapin

EARTHLY happiness is not dependent on the amount of one's possessions or the nature of one's employment.

—Charles W. Eliot

NOT only is it every man's privilege to be happy, it is his duty, his manifest obligation. Happiness is the condition of his higher achievements and his higher usefulness. It is the exhilaration of the highest energy and lends wings.

—Lilian Whiting

THE most completely lost of all days is the one on which we have not laughed.

HAPPINESS is rarely absent; it is we that know not its presence.

—Maurice Maeterlinck

IF it wasn't for the optimist, the pessimist would never know how happy he wasn't.

THE secret of happiness is—something to do.

—John Burroughs

INSTEAD of seeking happiness by going out of our place, our skill should be to find it where we are.

—Henry Ward Beecher

H E who has learned to laugh at himself is a near neighbor to happiness.

—W. M. Strickler

 BIDING happiness is not simply a possibility, but a duty...all may live above the troubles of life...worry is a poison and happiness a medicine.

—Newell Dwight Hillis

B EING happy—being appreciative, being grateful—is not altogether a matter of temperament. Nor is it dependent upon outward circumstances. Not at all.

—Ossian Lang

 IVE only in a great Today, whose happy thoughts weave golden hours.

—Josephine Rollett Wright

H APPY indeed the man who can say that he owes no man anything.

—Newell Dwight Hillis

M ORE hearts than we dream of enjoy our happiness and share our sorrow.

—George William Curtis

THE three arch-enemies of happiness: Hurry, Worry, and Debt.

—Newell Dwight Hillis

I BELIEVE in gittin' as much good outen life as you kin—not that I ever set out to look for happiness; seems like the folks that does, never find it. I jes' do the best I kin where the good Lord put me at, an' it looks like I got a happy feelin' in me 'most all the time.

—Mrs. Wiggs

DO not worry; eat three square meals a day; say your prayers; be courteous to your creditors; keep your digestion good; exercise; go slow and easy. Maybe there are other things that your special case requires to make you happy, but, my friend, these, I reckon, will give you a good lift.

—Abraham Lincoln

CHEERFULNESS accompanies patience, which is one of the main conditions of happiness and success in life.

—Samuel Smiles

THERE are two fundamental necessities for a happy life namely, a useful occupation for mind and body, and an outlet for unselfish affection.

—Henry D. Chapin

GET in the habit of looking for the silver lining in the cloud, and, when you have found it, continue to look at it rather than at the leaden gray in the middle. It will help you over many hated places.

BY forgetting ourselves in thinking of the feelings of others we gain happiness.

—Henry D. Chapin

IT is wonderful indeed how much innocent happiness we thoughtlessly throw away.

—Sir John Lubbock

LIVE on the sunny side; count everything joy; believe most thoroughly that all things are working for greater and greater good to you, and be determined to prove it in greater and greater measure.

—Christian D. Larson

HAPPINESS is not solitary, but social; and so we can never have it without sharing it with others.

—Henry van Dyke

THERE is no happiness in having and getting; but only in giving. Half the world is on the wrong scent in the pursuit of happiness.

—F. W. Gunsaulus

APPINESS is a pursuit to be followed as tirelessly as the pursuit of wisdom or of wealth.

—Newell Dwight Hillis

OW happiness consists in activity: such is the constitution of our nature: it is a running stream, and not a stagnant pool.

—J. M. Good

GRATEFUL heart is the mainspring of happiness.

—Ossian Lang

OY is not in things, it is in us, and I hold to the belief that the causes of our present unrest, of this contagious discontent spreading everywhere, are in us at least as much as in exterior conditions.

—Charles Wagner

OW the heart is so full that a drop over-fills it;
We are happy now because God wills it.

—Lowell

To make much of little, to find reasons of interest in common things, to develop a sensibility to mild enjoyments, to inspire the imagination, to throw a charm upon homely and familiar things, will constitute a man master of his own happiness.

—Henry Ward Beecher

The truly happy man is the man whose habits impose upon him the thinking of higher thoughts, dreaming the noblest dreams, exulting in the deepest joys.

—Newell Dwight Hillis

Beliefs we must have and must act on, and they are sure to affect profoundly our happiness in this world. How to treat our old beliefs and choose our new ones, with a view to happiness, is in these days a serious problem for every reflective person.

—Charles W. Eliot

Would you be happy, then from out your store
Carry good cheer to others; and the more
You give the more there still remains to give;
Cheer dies by hoarding, but when given doth live.

—Christopher Bannister

JUST BEING HAPPY

MAN is not simply a worker. If he is to be happy, he must also play.

—Newell Dwight Hillis

HAPPINESS, rightly understood, is the most desirable and the most important thing in life.

THAT thou art happy, owe to God. That thou continuest such, owe to thyself.

I CANNOT think but that the world would be better and brighter if our teachers would dwell on the Duty of Happiness as well as the Happiness of Duty.

—Sir John Lubbock

IN his own life, then, a man is not to expect happiness, only to profit by it gladly when it shall arise; he is on duty here; he knows not how or why, and does not need to know; he knows not for what hire, and must not ask. Somehow or other, though he does not know what goodness is, he must try to be good; somehow or other, though he cannot tell what will do it, he must try to give happiness to others.

—Robert Louis Stevenson

ERE'S hoping that on Fortune's face
You'll never see a frown,
And that the corners of your mouth
May never be turned down.

—Lucinda May

HAPPY man or woman is a better thing to find than a five-pound note. He or she is a radiating focus of good-will; and their entrance into a room is as though another candle had been lighted. We need not care whether they could prove the forty-seventh proposition; they do a better thing than that—they practically demonstrate the great Theorem of the Livableness of Life.

—Robert Louis Stevenson

O be a painter does it suffice to arm one's self with a brush, or does the purchase at great cost of a Stradivarius make one a musician? No more, if you had the whole paraphernalia of amusement in the perfection of its ingenuity, would it advance you upon your road to happiness. But with a bit of crayon a great artist makes an immortal sketch. It needs talent or genius to paint; and to amuse one's self the faculty of being happy, whoever possesses it, is amused at slight cost.

—Charles Wagner

N old proverb attributed happiness to him who expects little and thereby avoids disappointment

NO art, it may be said, was ever perfect, and not many noble, that has not been mirthfully conceived. And no man, it may be added, was ever anything but a wet blanket and a cross to his companions who boasted not a copious spirit of enjoyment.

—Robert Louis Stevenson

TALK happiness. Why, a well beggar has a better time of it than a sick king any day.

—Amber

TO attain the Art of Living is to attain happiness.

—Lilian Whiting

TO owe an obligation to a worthy friend is happiness.

—Pierce Chanon

A MAN who has a few friends, or one who has a dozen (if there be anyone so wealthy on this earth), cannot forget on how precarious a base his happiness reposes; and how by a stroke or two of fate—a death, a few light words, a piece of stamped paper, or a woman's bright eyes—he may be left in a month destitute of all.

—Robert Louis Stevenson

FOR Yesterday is but a Dream,
And Tomorrow is only a Vision;
But Today, well lived,
Makes every Yesterday
A dream of Happiness,
And every Tomorrow a Vision of Hope.

LABOR, the symbol of man's punishment;
Labor, the secret of man's happiness.

—James Montgomery

GENTLENESS and cheerfulness, these come before all morality; they are the perfect duties. If your morals make you dreary, depend upon it they are wrong. I do not say "Give them up," for they may be all you have; but conceal them like vice, lest they should spoil the lives of better and simpler people.

—Robert Louis Stevenson

IF you are happy, it is largely to your own credit. If you are miserable, it is chiefly your own fault.

—William DeWitt Hyde

IT is the initial business and purpose of life to be happy; and, lest the moralist should object to this as a frivolous proposition, it may be added that it is that true happiness synonymous with holiness—which is meant—the quality of happiness that manifests itself in abounding energy and goodwill.

—Lilian Whiting

IT is one of the paths to success and happiness in life, or rather it *is* success and happiness in itself, to be swiftly responsive to the angel when he draws near.

—Lilian Whiting

HAPPINESS, like health, is the normal state; and when this is not felt, the cause should be looked for just as in illness the cause should be scrutinized and removed.

—Lilian Whiting

HAPPINESS is neither within us nor without us. It is the union of ourselves with God.

—Pascal

BE good and you will be happy—but you may be lonesome.

THE happiest heart that ever beat
Was in some quiet breast,
That found the common daylight sweet,
And left to Heaven the rest.
—John Vance Cheney

HAPPINESS and goodness, according to canting moralists, stand in the relation of effect and cause. There was never anything less proved or less probable: our happiness is never in our own hands; we inherit our constitutions; we stand buffet among friends and enemies; we may be so built as to feel a sneer or an aspersion with unusual keenness, and so circumstanced as to be unusually exposed to them; we may have nerves very sensitive to pain, and be afflicted with a disease more painful. Virtue will not help us, and it is not meant to help us. It is not even its own reward, except for the self-centered and—I had almost said—the unamiable.
—Robert Louis Stevenson

GOD has given us tongues that we may say something pleasant to our fellow-men.
—Heinrich Heine

HAPPINESS is a great love and a much serving.
—Olive Schreiner

F a person cannot be happy without remaining idle, idle he should remain. It is a revolutionary precept; but, thanks to hunger and the workhouse, one not easily to be abused; and, within practical limits, it is one of the most incontestable truths in the whole Body of Morality. Look at one of your industrious fellows for a moment, I beseech you. He sows hurry and reaps indigestion; he puts a vast deal of activity out to interest, and receives a large measure of nervous derangement in return. Either he absents himself entirely from all fellowship, and lives a recluse in a garret, with carpet slippers and a leaden inkpot; or he comes among people swiftly and bitterly, in a contraction of his whole nervous system, to discharge some temper before he returns to work. I do not care how much or how well he works, this fellow is an evil feature in other people's lives. They would be happier if he were dead.

—Robert Louis Stevenson

ET us hope that one day all mankind will be happy and wise; and, though this day never should dawn, to have hoped for it cannot be wrong. And, in any event it is helpful to speak of happiness to those who are sad, that thus at least they may learn what it is that happiness means.

—Maurice Maeterlinck

HE happiest women, like the happiest nations, have no history.

—George Eliot

MY DEAR ROBERT—One passage in your Letter a little displeased me...You say that "this world to you seems drained of all its sweets!" At first I had hoped you only meant to insinuate the high price of Sugar! but I am afraid you meant more. O Robert, I don't know what you call sweet. Honey and the honeycomb, roses and violets, are yet in the earth. The sun and moon yet reign in Heaven, and the lesser lights keep up their pretty twinklings. Meats and drinks, sweet sights and sweet smells, a country walk, spring and autumn, follies and repentance, quarrels and reconcilements, have all a sweetness by turns. So good humor and good nature, friends at home that love you, and friends abroad that miss you—you possess all these things, and more innumerable; and these are all sweet things. You may extract honey from everything; do not go a-gathering after gall...I assure you I find this world a very pretty place.

—Charles Lamb to Robert Lloyd

SOME work to do, something to care for, and something to hope for, are what make happiness in life.

—Dr. Chalmers

ALL true happiness is both a consequence and a cause of life; it is a sign of its vigor, and a source of its continuance.

—John Ruskin

ONE of the greatest arts in life, and one of the most neglected, is that of finding happiness in little things.

ALL real and wholesome enjoyments possible to man have been just as possible to him, since first he was made of the earth, as they are now; and they are possible to him chiefly in peace. To watch the corn grow, and the blossoms set; to draw hard breath over ploughshare or spade; to read, to think, to love, to hope, to pray—these are the things that make men happy.

—John Ruskin

LOOK within. Within is the fountain of happiness, and it will ever bubble up if thou wilt but dig.

—Marcus Aurelius

I USED to think it was great to disregard happiness, to press to a high goal, careless, disdainful of it. But now I see that there is nothing so great as to be capable of happiness—to pluck it out of each moment; and, whatever happens, to find that one can ride as gay and buoyant on the angry, menacing, tumultuous waves of life as on those that glide and glitter under a clear sky; that it is not defeat and wretchedness which come out of the storms of adversity, but strength and calmness and joy.

—A. Gilchrist

ARE you awfully tired with play, little girl;
  Weary, discouraged and sick?
I'll tell you the loviest game in the world—
  Do something for somebody, quick!

HOW soon a smile of God can change the world!
  How we are made for happiness—how work
Grows play, adversity a winning fight!
  —Robert Browning

WONDROUS is the strength of cheerfulness, altogether past cal-
culation its powers of endurance. Efforts, to be permanently
useful, must be uniformly joyous—a spirit all sunshine, graceful
from very gladness, beautiful because bright.

—Thomas Carlyle

HAPPINESS does not consist in possessing much, but in hoping
and loving much.

—Lamennais

THE happiness of life is made up of minute fractions—countless
infinitesimals of pleasurable thought and genial feeling.

—Samuel Taylor Coleridge

CHEERINESS is a thing to be more profoundly grateful for than all that genius ever inspired or talent ever accomplished. Next best to natural, spontaneous cheeriness, is deliberate, intended and persistent cheeriness, which we can create, can cultivate and can so foster and cherish that after a few years the world will never suspect that it was not an hereditary gift.

—Helen Hunt Jackson

JOY does not happen. It is the inevitable result of certain lines followed and laws obeyed, and so a matter of character.

—Maltbie D. Babcock

IT is an everlasting duty—the duty of being brave.

—Thomas Carlyle

IF you want to be happy, do not try to live more than one day at a time.

JOY is the mainspring in the whole round of everlasting Nature; Joy moves the wheels of the great timepiece of the world; she it is that loosens flowers from their buds, suns from their firmaments, rolling spheres in distant spaces not seen by the glass of the astronomer.

—Schiller

*P*OWER dwells with cheerfulness.

—Emerson

*H*APPY is the man who sees
The stars shine through his cypress trees.

—Lowell

*T*HIS instinct for happiness is as deeply imbedded in man's nature as the instinct of life itself.

—Newell Dwight Hillis

*I*T is a happy thing for us that this is really all we have to concern ourselves about—what to do next. No man can do the second thing. He can do the first.

—George Macdonald

*M*ANKIND are always happier for having been happy. So that if you make them happy now, you make them happy twenty years hence by the memory of it.

—Sidney Smith

*W*E should be as happy as possible, and our happiness should last as long as possible; for those who can finally issue from self by the portal of happiness know infinitely wider freedom than those who pass through the gate of sadness.

—Maurice Maeterlinck